WOULD YOU RATHER?
CHRISTMAS EDITION

COPYRIGHT © 2019 BIG DREAMS ART SUPPLIES
BIGDREAMSARTSUPPLIES.com
BOOK DESIGN: DAVOR RATKOVIC
PRINTED IN THE UNITED STATE OF AMERICA

WOULD YOU RATHER...

IT RAINED MARSHMALLOWS
ON CHRISTMAS

OR

REGULAR SNOW THAT YOU
COULD SLED ON AND BUILD
SNOWMEN OUT OF?

HAVE YOUR BIRTHDAY
BE ON CHRISTMAS

OR

SHARE YOUR BIRTHDAY WITH
YOUR BROTHERS AND SISTERS?

WOULD YOU RATHER...

HAVE A REINDEER FOR A PET

OR

AN ELF THAT
CLEANS YOUR ROOM?

SING CHRISTMAS CAROLS
WHILE YOU GO
TRICK-OR-TREATING ON HALLOWEEN

OR

WEAR YOUR HALLOWEEN
COSTUME AT CHRISTMAS?

WOULD YOU RATHER...

DRIVE THE POLAR EXPRESS

OR

FLY SANTA'S SLEIGH?

SPEND CHRISTMAS WITH YOUR FAVORITE MOVIE CHARACTER

OR

YOUR FAVORITE TV CHARACTER?

Xavier Riddle

WOULD YOU RATHER...

HAVE COOKIES AND MILK
LEFT OUT IF YOU
WERE SANTA CLAUS

✓

OR

PIZZA AND COKE?

HAVE A FANCY
CHRISTMAS DINNER

✓

OR

EAT CHRISTMAS KENTUCKY
FRIED CHICKEN, WHICH IS A BIG
TRADITION IN JAPAN?

WOULD YOU RATHER...

CHRISTMAS BE
IN THE SUMMER

OR

IN THE WINTER?

BE STRANDED ON A DESERTED
ISLAND WITH SANTA
WHO HAS FRUIT CAKE TO EAT

OR

THE EASTER BUNNY
WHO HAS CARROT CAKE?

WOULD YOU RATHER...

HAVE A CHOCOLATE EATING CONTEST WITH ELVES

OR

A DONUT EATING CONTEST WITH SANTA?

FROSTY THE SNOWMAN BE YOUR SCHOOL'S PRINCIPAL

OR

OLAF?

WOULD YOU RATHER...

WELCOME CHRISTMAS WITH
COLORFUL PAPER LANTERNS,
JUGGLERS AND ACROBATS
LIKE THEY DO IN CHINA

OR

✓ WITH FIREWORKS AND
HUGE ELECTRIC CHRISTMAS TREES
LIKE THEY DO IN BRAZIL?

SHOVEL SNOW ALL DAY

OR

HAVE TO LISTEN TO THE
"RUDOLPH THE RED NOSED
REINDEER" SONG ALL DAY?

WOULD YOU RATHER...

STEP BAREFOOT
ON CHRISTMAS LIGHTS

OR

ON CHRISTMAS
EDITION LEGO'S?

BE AN ELF
WORKING ALL DAY

OR

THE GRINCH
ON VACATION?

WOULD YOU RATHER...

STAR IN A TERRIBLE
BUT POPULAR
CHRISTMAS MOVIE

OR

ONE THAT IS GREAT BUT
NOBODY KNOWS ABOUT?

THE ABOMINABLE
SNOWMAN ATTACK
YOUR HOUSE ON CHRISTMAS EVE

OR

THE GRINCH COME TO
STEAL ALL YOUR PRESENTS

WOULD YOU RATHER...

KNOW EXACTLY
WHAT YOU'LL GET
FOR CHRISTMAS EVERY YEAR

OR

KNOW WHAT
EVERYONE ELSE WANTS?

HAVE BIG ELF EARS
FOR CHRISTMAS VACATION

OR

REINDEER ANTLERS?

WOULD YOU RATHER...

SING CHRISTMAS SONGS LIKE GOOFY

OR

DONALD DUCK?

INVITE YOUR WORST ENEMY TO CHRISTMAS DINNER

OR

TELL YOUR WHOLE FAMILY YOUR MOST EMBARRASSING SECRETS?

WOULD YOU RATHER...

GET LOST IN A CANDY CANE FOREST

OR

A CHRISTMAS SPRINKLE DESERT?

UNTANGLE 100 STRANDS OF CHRISTMAS LIGHTS

OR

WRAP 100 PRESENTS?

WOULD YOU RATHER...

CHUG A BOWL
FULL OF EGGNOG

OR

A BOWL FULL
OF HOT CHOCOLATE?

TAKE A BITE OF A SUPER HOT,
CHRISTMAS COOKIE
JUST OUT OF THE OVEN

OR

EAT A SUPER COLD ICICLE?

WOULD YOU RATHER...

LIVE IN A GINGERBREAD HOUSE WITH A MARSHMALLOW BED

OR

TAKE BATHS EVERY DAY IN HOT CHOCOLATE?

HAVE A SNOW STORM EVERY DAY IN DECEMBER

OR

NO SNOW FOR CHRISTMAS?

WOULD YOU RATHER...

FORGET WHO GAVE YOU YOUR CHRISTMAS PRESENTS

OR

HAVE NOBODY REMEMBER WHAT YOU GAVE THEM?

HAVE A BIG BELLY LIKE SANTA CLAUS

OR

A BIG WHITE BEARD?

HANG YOUR STOCKINGS BY THE CHIMNEY WITH CARE

OR

SET YOUR SHOES BY THE BACK DOOR TO BE FILLED WITH TREATS LIKE THEY DO IN FRANCE AND THE NETHERLANDS?

GO FOR A RIDE ON SANTA'S SLEIGH

OR

GET ALL OF THE CANDY IN IT?

WOULD YOU RATHER...

GET STUCK IN A
CHIMNEY FOR AN HOUR

OR

LOST IN A SNOW STORM
FOR AN HOUR?

HAVE A CHRISTMAS TREE THAT
NEVER STOPS COMPLAINING
ABOUT BEING CUT DOWN

OR

A GINGERBREAD MAN WHO NEVER
STOPS TELLING YOU
HOW HORRIBLE PEOPLE ARE
FOR EATING THEM?

WOULD YOU RATHER...

BE THE MAYOR OF WHOVILLE
IN THE GRINCH MOVIE

OR

BE THE PRINCIPAL
OF YOUR SCHOOL?

YOUR PARENTS
HATE CHRISTMAS

OR

BE COMPLETELY OBSESSED
WITH IT AND IT'S THE ONLY
THING THEY EVER TALK ABOUT?

**BE A CHARACTER IN
THE RUDOLPH MOVIE**

OR

CHARLIE BROWN'S CHRISTMAS?

**CLEAN OUT SANTA'S
REINDEER BARN**

OR

**CLEAN OUT
THE ELVES' BATHROOM?**

WOULD YOU RATHER...

**HAVE TO WEAR AN
ELF COSTUME ON CHRISTMAS**

— OR —

**HAVE A WEIRD HAIRCUT
THAT WAS COLORED
RED AND GREEN?**

**FILL YOUR NOSE AND
EARS WITH MARSHMALLOWS**

— OR —

**TRY TO STUFF 100
LITTLE MARSHMALLOWS
IN YOUR MOUTH?**

YOUR DOG ATE YOUR VERY
IMPORTANT HOMEWORK

OR

ONE OF YOUR
CHRISTMAS PRESENTS?

NEVER KNOW WHAT
YOU'RE GETTING
FOR CHRISTMAS EACH YEAR

OR

YOU CAN PICK WHAT YOU GET
EACH YEAR, BUT EVERYTHING
ARRIVES COVERED IN JELLO?

WOULD YOU RATHER...

HAVE THE GHOST OF CHRISTMAS PAST TAKE YOU INTO THE PAST AND LEAVE YOU THERE SO YOU HAVE TO RELIVE EVERYTHING

OR

HAVE THE GHOST OF CHRISTMAS FUTURE SHOW YOU THAT WHEN YOU GET OLDER, YOUR BOSS IS EBENEZER SCROOGE?

HAVE TO WEAR A HAT COVERED IN BLINKING CHRISTMAS LIGHTS AT SCHOOL

OR

BE THE ONLY KID WHO WASN'T WEARING CHRISTMAS CLOTHES AT SCHOOL?

WOULD YOU RATHER...

WAKE UP CHRISTMAS MORNING AS A GINGERBREAD BOY OR GIRL

OR

A SNOWMAN?

LIVE WITH SANTA AT THE NORTH POLE

OR

WITH MICKEY MOUSE AT HIS CLUBHOUSE?

WOULD YOU RATHER...

HAVE REALLY LOUD NEIGHBORS
WHO LOVE TO SING CHRISTMAS
CAROLS ALL NIGHT LONG

OR

HAVE GRUMPY NEIGHBORS
WHO YELL BAH HUMBUG
AND HATE CHRISTMAS?

DANCE IN THE NUTCRACKER
BALLET AS THE RAT KING

OR

A TOY SOLDIER?

WOULD YOU RATHER...

BE RULER OF THE ABOMINABLE SNOWMEN WHO DON'T LIKE CHRISTMAS

OR

BE THE LOWLIEST ELF IN SANTA'S WORKSHOP?

HAVE A UNICORN HORN

OR

RUDOLPH'S NOSE?

WOULD YOU RATHER...

BE KIDNAPPED BY CHRISTMAS FAIRIES

OR

OLAF THE SNOWMAN?

HAVE ELSA'S POWERS FROM FROZEN THAT YOU CAN'T CONTROL

OR

BE ABLE TO MAKE IT RAIN SPRINKLES ANYTIME YOU WANT?

WOULD YOU RATHER...

RIDE TO SCHOOL IN A CAR
WRAPPED UP LIKE A CHRISTMAS
PRESENT ONE MORNING

OR

HAVE YOUR PARENTS PLAY
CHRISTMAS MUSIC REALLY
LOUDLY WHILE THEY DROP
YOU OFF EVERY DAY FOR A WEEK?

DO THE NUTCRACKER BALLET
ALONE IN FRONT OF YOUR CLASS
(IN A TUTU)

OR

LET YOUR WHOLE CLASS
BLAST YOU WITH SNOWBALLS

WOULD YOU RATHER...

SNEAK A PHOTO OF SANTA DELIVERING PRESENTS AND PROVE HE EXISTS TO THE WORLD, THUS MAKING YOU RICH AND FAMOUS, BUT SANTA CAN NO LONGER DELIVER PRESENTS

OR

NEVER CATCH HIM DELIVERING PRESENTS AND CHRISTMAS CONTINUES LIKE NORMAL

WATCH "HOW THE GRINCH STOLE CHRISTMAS" 50 TIMES BACK TO BACK

OR

NEVER BE ABLE TO SEE ANOTHER CHRISTMAS MOVIE AGAIN

WOULD YOU RATHER...

**HAVE TO WAIT AN
EXTRA WEEK TO OPEN
YOUR CHRISTMAS PRESENTS**

— OR —

**JUST GET HALF OF
YOUR PRESENTS BUT GET
THEM ON CHRISTMAS DAY**

**HAVE YOUR HEAD SWITCHED
WITH A SNOWMAN'S HEAD,
BUT NORMAL HUMAN BODY**

— OR —

**HAVE A SNOWMAN'S BODY,
BUT YOUR REGULAR
HEAD ON TOP**

WOULD YOU RATHER...

DECORATE YOUR TREE
WITH CHRISTMAS
ORNAMENTS AND TINSEL

OR

GOOD LUCK SPIDER WEBS
LIKE THEY DO IN THE UKRAINE?

SLOWLY HAVE YOUR BODY
GROW TO THE SIZE AND SHAPE
OF SANTA (INCLUDING BEARD)

OR

SLOWLY HAVE YOUR BODY
SHRINK DOWN TO THE SIZE
AND SHAPE OF AN ELF

WOULD YOU RATHER...

HAVE TO WAIT AN EXTRA
DAY FOR CHRISTMAS THIS YEAR

—————— OR ——————

GO RIGHT BACK TO SCHOOL
THE DAY AFTER CHRISTMAS?

HAVE REINDEER
HOOVES FOR FEET

—————— OR ——————

HAVE REGULAR
HANDS AS YOUR FEET

WOULD YOU RATHER...

BECOME A SUPERHERO WHOSE
ONLY POWER IS THAT YOU CAN
TURN INTO A GINGERBREAD MAN

OR

BE ABLE TO FLY, BUT ONLY
WHEN YOU ARE DRESSED UP
LIKE A REINDEER?

SANTA COMES DOWN YOUR
CHIMNEY IN HIS WARM, RED SUIT

OR

TRADES HIS SUIT FOR
COOLER SUMMER CLOTHES
LIKE HE DOES IN AUSTRALIA?

WOULD YOU RATHER...

EVERY DAY BE CHRISTMAS

OR

YOUR BIRTHDAY?

HAVE A CROWD OF PEOPLE
IN YOUR YARD YELLING
MERRY CHRISTMAS AT YOU

OR

SOMEONE CALLING YOUR HOUSE
EVERY FEW MINUTES TO
WISH YOU A MERRY CHRISTMAS?

WOULD YOU RATHER...

LIVE ON THE ISLAND OF
MISFIT TOYS AND
GO TO PARTIES ALL THE TIME

OR

BE THEIR RULER BUT NOT
GET INVITED TO ANY PARTIES
BECAUSE YOU'RE NORMAL?

EAT CHRISTMAS COOKIES
FOR BREAKFAST EVERY
DAY IN DECEMBER

OR

GET HOT CHOCOLATE
AND CANDY CANES
AS AN AFTER SCHOOL SNACK?

WOULD YOU RATHER...

HELP SANTA DELIVER
PRESENTS ON CHRISTMAS EVE

OR

VISIT THE NORTH POLE
AND LEARN HOW THE ELVES
MAKE ALL THE TOYS?

LIVE IN A SMALL
GINGERBREAD HOUSE

OR

IN A GIANT ICE PALACE?

WOULD YOU RATHER...

HAVE FROSTY THE SNOWMAN
AS YOUR BEST FRIEND

•——————— OR ———————•

ELF (FROM THE MOVIE)?

SPEND THE DAY PLAYING
SILLY TRICKS ON THE GRINCH

•——————— OR ———————•

HELPING ON THE ISLAND
OF MISFIT TOYS?

WOULD YOU RATHER...

HAVE A DAD ON
SANTA'S NAUGHTY LIST

OR

A DAD WHO EMBARRASSES
YOU EVERY CHRISTMAS
IN FRONT OF YOUR FRIENDS?

SPEND THE DAY WITH AN ELF ON
THE SHELF KEEPING TRACK
OF WHO IS NICE AND NAUGHTY

OR

SPEND THE DAY WITH A NISSE,
A CHRISTMAS GNOME FROM
NORWAY THAT SOMETIMES PLAYS
TRICKS ON NAUGHTY PEOPLE?

WOULD YOU RATHER...

DECORATE YOUR CHRISTMAS
TREE WITH COLORFUL
ORNAMENTS YOU MAKE YOURSELF

OR

STORE BOUGHT ORNAMENTS
ALL IN ONE COLOR?

SWIM IN A GIANT
POOL OF GREEN JELLO

OR

MARSHMALLOWS?

WOULD YOU RATHER...

WEAR CURLY ELF SHOES TO SCHOOL

OR

A POINTY ELF HAT?

RIDE IN A ONE HORSE OPEN SLEIGH

OR

ROCK AROUND THE CHRISTMAS TREE?

WOULD YOU RATHER...

HAVE TO SING JINGLE BELLS
ON THE ANNOUNCEMENTS
AT SCHOOL

OR

HAVE TO LISTEN TO
JINGLE BELLS PLAYED OVER
THE INTERCOM ALL DAY?

EAT TRADITIONAL CHRISTMAS
TURKEY DINNER

OR

TACOS?

WOULD YOU RATHER...

YOUR HOUSE SMELL
LIKE CANDY CANES

•——————— OR ———————•

FRESHLY BAKED COOKIES?

SANTA LEAVE YOU ONE BIG
PRESENT YOU REALLY WANT

•——————— OR ———————•

A BUNCH OF AWESOME
SURPRISE PRESENTS?

WOULD YOU RATHER...

EAT A WHOLE FRUITCAKE

— OR —

EAT A BUCKET OF CHRISTMAS SPRINKLES?

HAVE AN ELF THAT WRAPS ALL YOUR PRESENTS FOR YOU

— OR —

AN ELF THAT HELPS YOU WITH YOUR HOMEWORK?

WOULD YOU RATHER...

FEAST ON DONUTS

OR

A YULE LOG CAKE WHICH IS A CHOCOLATE AND CREAM CAKE SERVED IN MANY EUROPEAN COUNTRIES?

DANCE LIKE A SUGAR PLUM FAIRY

OR

MARCH LIKE A TOY SOLDIER?

WOULD YOU RATHER...

GET COAL IN YOUR STOCKING

OR

A POTATO LIKE
NAUGHTY CHILDREN IN
THE NETHERLANDS?

BE VISITED BY THE GHOST
OF CHRISTMAS PAST

OR

THE GHOST OF
CHRISTMAS FUTURE?

WOULD YOU RATHER...

GIVE THE PERFECT PRESENT TO SOMEONE YOU LOVE

OR

GET THE PRESENT YOU WANT THE MOST?

GET TO SPEND CHRISTMAS IN YOUR JAMMIES ALL DAY

OR

WEAR A FANCY CHRISTMAS OUTFIT TO A SPECIAL PARTY?

WOULD YOU RATHER...

ROAR LIKE A POLAR BEAR
WHEN YOU'RE HAPPY

●————————— OR —————————●

BARK LIKE A SEAL
WHEN YOU LAUGH?

HAVE YOUR CHRISTMAS TREE
INSIDE YOUR HOUSE

●————————— OR —————————●

AN OUTSIDE CHRISTMAS TREE
THAT IS THE HOME
TO TALKING ANIMALS?

**EAT A CARROT
FLAVORED CANDY CANE**

OR

**A CANDY CANE
FLAVORED CARROT?**

**DECORATE THE TOP
OF YOUR CHRISTMAS TREE
WITH AN ANGEL**

OR

A TROLL WITH CRAZY HAIR?

WOULD YOU RATHER...

WALK AROUND YOUR NEIGHBORHOOD SINGING CHRISTMAS CAROLS

OR

MARCH AROUND AS THE LITTLE DRUMMER BOY?

HAVE A CARROT NOSE

OR

BUTTON EYES?

WOULD YOU RATHER...

HAVE YOUR CHRISTMAS PRESENT
DELIVERED IN A GIANT BOX WITH
NO WRAPPING PAPER

OR

A SMALL BOX THAT
IS BEAUTIFULLY WRAPPED?

SEND CHRISTMAS CARDS
WITH A PICTURE WHERE
YOUR WHOLE FAMILY
IS WEARING THEIR PAJAMAS

OR

YOUR WHOLE FAMILY
IS DRESSED UP AS REINDEER?

WOULD YOU RATHER...

FIND THE PERFECT
CHRISTMAS PRESENT FOR
YOUR BROTHER OR SISTER

OR

THE PERFECT PRESENT
FOR YOUR PET?

PLAY REINDEER GAMES
WITH RUDOLPH

OR

HAVE A SNOWBALL FIGHT WITH
FROSTY AND HIS FRIENDS?

WOULD YOU RATHER...

HAVE TO WRAP CHRISTMAS
PRESENTS WITH NO SCISSORS

OR

NO TAPE?

BE THE CREATOR OF THE WORLDS
BEST GINGERBREAD HOUSE

OR

THE DECORATOR OF THE WORLDS
PRETTIEST CHRISTMAS TREE?

WOULD YOU RATHER...

DECORATE YOUR CHRISTMAS TREE WITH STINKY SOCKS

OR

BANANA PEELS?

WEAR YOUR PAJAMAS TO CHRISTMAS DINNER

OR

AN UGLY CHRISTMAS SWEATER?

WOULD YOU RATHER...

KISS THE ABOMINABLE
SNOWMAN UNDER
THE MISTLETOE

OR

THE GRINCH?

SANTA DRIVE YOU TO
SCHOOL IN HIS SLEIGH

OR

A FANCY LIMOUSINE?

WOULD YOU RATHER...

WEAR A SHIRT WITH BRIGHT
BLINKING CHRISTMAS LIGHTS

—————— OR ——————

LOUD JINGLE BELLS?

HAVE A HERD OF FLYING CATS
GUIDE YOUR SLEIGH IF
YOU WERE SANTA CLAUS

—————— OR ——————

A HERD OF
FLYING ELEPHANTS?

WOULD YOU RATHER...

DECORATE A CHRISTMAS PALM
TREE INSTEAD OF A NORMAL ONE

OR

A CHRISTMAS CACTUS?

LEAD THE CHRISTMAS
PARADE AT THE NORTH POLE

OR

DISNEY WORLD?

WOULD YOU RATHER...

HAVE TO COOK EVERYONE CHRISTMAS DINNER

OR

DO ALL THE DISHES AFTER CHRISTMAS DINNER IS OVER?

HAND MAKE 10 BEAUTIFUL CHRISTMAS CARDS TO SEND TO YOUR CLOSEST FRIENDS

OR

SIGN YOUR NAME TO FIFTY CHRISTMAS CARDS TO SEND TO EVERYONE YOU KNOW?

WOULD YOU RATHER...

HAVE AN ADVENT CALENDAR
THAT GIVES YOU $1 EACH
DAY UNTIL CHRISTMAS

OR

A BIG PIECE OF
CANDY EACH DAY?

GO TO A CHRISTMAS TREE FARM
AND CUT DOWN A SMALL,
BUT PRETTY TREE TO
DECORATE WITH YOUR FAMILY

OR

HAVE SOMEONE ELSE SELECT AND
DECORATE A GIANT CHRISTMAS
TREE FOR YOUR HOUSE?

WOULD YOU RATHER...

**BE THE BEST
ICE SKATER ON THE RINK**

OR

**WIN A SNOWBALL FIGHT
AGAINST THE SCHOOL BULLY?**

**EXCHANGE A TINY
PRESENT WITH
EACH OF YOUR CLASSMATES**

OR

**EXCHANGE ONE BIG PRESENT
WITH YOUR BEST FRIEND?**

DECORATE A GINGERBREAD HOUSE
THAT LOOKS SO AMAZING THAT
EVERYONE KEEPS TRYING TO EAT IT

OR

DECORATE A GINGERBREAD HOUSE
THAT ISN'T VERY GOOD
SO NOBODY NOTICES IT?

RIDE IN A ONE-HORSE
OPEN SLEIGH TO GO LOOK
AT CHRISTMAS LIGHTS

OR

A WARM, COZY CAR?

WOULD YOU RATHER...

FIND A CROAKY FROG LIVING IN
YOUR CHRISTMAS TREE

OR

A SQUEAKY CHIPMUNK?

SPEND A LONG TIME MAKING THE
PERFECT CHRISTMAS PRESENT FOR
SOMEONE THAT THEY WILL LOVE

OR

SPEND JUST A MINUTE
AND ORDER SOMETHING
ONLINE THAT'S JUST OKAY?

WOULD YOU RATHER...

YOUR SECRET SANTA GIVE YOU
A BOX OF YOUR FAVORITE CANDY

—— OR ——

A TIN FILLED WITH
YOUR FAVORITE COOKIES?

GET FIVE GOLDEN RINGS
FOR CHRISTMAS

—— OR ——

A PARTRIDGE IN
A PEAR TREE?

WOULD YOU RATHER...

HAVE A CHRISTMAS COOKIE
SWAP WITH FRIENDS

—————— OR ——————

SPEND ALL DAY BAKING,
DECORATING AND EATING
COOKIES WITH YOUR FAMILY?

SPEND THE EVENING
WATCHING CHRISTMAS MOVIES

—————— OR ——————

GO CHRISTMAS CAROLING
IN YOUR NEIGHBORHOOD?

WOULD YOU RATHER...

WRITE THE PERFECT LETTER TO SANTA, BUT HAVE TO READ IT IN FRONT OF YOUR WHOLE CLASS

OR

FORGET TO WRITE A LETTER TO SANTA AND WORRY THAT HE WON'T BRING WHAT YOU WANT?

SHRINK AND LIVE FOR A DAY IN A TINY CHRISTMAS VILLAGE

OR

TURN INTO A CHRISTMAS GIANT FOR A DAY?

WOULD YOU RATHER...

BE EBENEZER SCROOGE

OR

THE NICE GUY WHO WORKS FOR HIM WITH A LOVING FAMILY BUT IS VERY POOR?

LICK A COLD FLAG POLE AND GET YOUR TONGUE STUCK

OR

WEAR A FUZZY PINK BUNNY SUIT LIKE RALPH IN A CHRISTMAS STORY?

WOULD YOU RATHER...

EAT A BIG BOWL
OF CRANBERRY SAUCE

— OR —

A BIG BOWL OF
FIGGY PUDDING?

BE FORGOTTEN AND LEFT
HOME ALONE ON CHRISTMAS

— OR —

GO ON A TRIP ALL BY
YOURSELF FOR CHRISTMAS?

WOULD YOU RATHER...

HAVE FINGERNAILS THAT
LIGHT UP LIKE CHRISTMAS LIGHTS
WHEN YOU'RE NERVOUS

OR

EYES THAT LIGHT UP
LIKE CHRISTMAS LIGHTS
WHEN YOU'RE HAPPY?

BE A SECRET SANTA WHO GIVES
NICE, THOUGHTFUL PRESENTS

OR

ONE WHO PLAYS SILLY,
NAUGHTY PRANKS?

WOULD YOU RATHER...

TAKE A PLANE TO AN EXOTIC CHRISTMAS VACATION

OR

GO ON A CHRISTMAS CRUISE?

INVITE YOUR CURRENT TEACHER OVER FOR CHRISTMAS DINNER

OR

THE TEACHER YOU HAD LAST YEAR?

WOULD YOU RATHER...

FROSTY THE SNOWMAN WOKE
YOU UP WITH A SNOWBALL
IN YOUR FACE ON CHRISTMAS

OR

RUDOLPH NUDGES YOU
AWAKE WITH HIS ANTLERS?

HAVE A SNOWBALL
FOR A HEAD

OR

ICICLES FOR TEETH?

WOULD YOU RATHER...

RIDE A REINDEER
TO SCHOOL IN THE SNOW

OR

ON A CAMEL
THROUGH THE DESERT?

SANTA SHAVE HIS BEARD

OR

GO ON A DIET AND
BECOME SUPER SKINNY?

WOULD YOU RATHER...

**CELEBRATE CHRISTMAS
WITH A YULE CAT LIKE
THEY DO IN ICELAND**

OR

**WITH A GIANT STRAW
YULE GOAT AS
THEY DO IN SWEDEN?**

**HAVE A BAND THAT FOLLOWS
YOU AROUND PLAYING
CHRISTMAS MUSIC**

OR

**A BAND THAT PLAYS SONGS
YOU LIKE, BUT THE BAND
IS NOT VERY GOOD?**

WOULD YOU RATHER...

GO SNOW SKIING

OR

BOBSLEDDING?

RIDE IN A LIMOUSINE TO
CHRISTMAS FESTIVITIES

OR

USE ROLLER SKATES
LIKE MANY PEOPLE DO IN
CARACAS, VENEZUELA?

WOULD YOU RATHER...

EAT 100 CANDY CANES

●——————— OR ———————●

ONLY GET CANDY CANES
IN YOUR STOCKING

BE GIVEN A JINGLE BELL
FROM ONE OF
SANTA'S REINDEER HARNESSES

●——————— OR ———————●

BE GIVEN A HAT FROM
SANTA'S BEST ELF HELPER?

WOULD YOU RATHER...

**HAVE TO DO KARAOKE TO ROCKIN'
AROUND THE CHRISTMAS TREE**

OR

**ALL I WANT FOR CHRISTMAS
IS MY TWO FRONT TEETH?**

**SLED DOWN A BIG SNOWY
HILL IN YOUR BATHING SUIT**

OR

**SLIDE DOWN A GIANT WATER
SLIDE IN A SANTA SUIT?**

WOULD YOU RATHER...

BE DRIVEN AROUND TOWN
BY THE GRINCH IN A LIMOUSINE

OR

SANTA IN A GARBAGE TRUCK?

GET AN AWESOME WOULD YOU
RATHER BOOK FOR CHRISTMAS

OR

A SWEATER?

WOULD YOU RATHER...

GO TO SCHOOL
FOR ALL OF CHRISTMAS
VACATION AND CHRISTMAS DAY

OR

GO TO SCHOOL ALL SUMMER?

EAT A CANDY CANE DIPPED
IN CHOCOLATE COVERED ANTS

OR

EAT ICE CREAM
MIXED WITH LADYBUGS?

YOUR REVIEW

WHAT IF I TOLD YOU THAT JUST ONE MINUTE OUT OF YOUR LIFE COULD GIVE US AN ENORMOUS BOOST? WHAT AM I YAPPING ABOUT? I'M TALING ABOUT LEAVING THIS BOOK A REVIEW.

I PROMISE YOU, WE TAKE THEM VERY SERIOUSLY.

DON'T BELIEVE ME?

EACH TIME RIGHT AFTER SOMEONE JUST LIKE YOU LEAVES THIS BOOK A REVIEW, A LITTLE SIREN GOES OFF RIGHT HERE IN OUR OFFICE. EVEN OUR NEIGHBORS CAN HEAR IT, AND A BIG OLE GRIN SHOWS UP ON EVERYONE'S FACE.

A DISCO BALL POPS OUT OF THE CEILING, FLASHING LIGHTS COME ON... AND IT'S PARTY TIME!

ROGER, OUR MARKETING OFFICER ALWAYS AND I MEAN ALWAYS, STARTS FLOSSING AND KEEPS IT UP FOR AWHILE. HE'S PRETTY GOOD AT IT. (IT'S A DANCE, NOT SOMETHING HE DOES WITH HIS TEETH)

SARAH, OUR OFFICE BOSS RUNS OUTSIDE AND GIVES EVERYONE ON THE STREET HIGH FIVES.

OUR EDITORS HAVE A SECTION UPSTAIRS WHERE THEY WORK AND WHEN THE REVIEW SIREN GOES OFF THEY ALL HOP IN THE SWIRLY SLIDE AND RIDE DOWN TO A GIANT PIT OF MARSHMALLOWS WHERE THEY ROLL AROUND AND MAKE MARSHMALLOW ANGELS.

IT'S ALL A PRETTY BIG DEAL FOR US.

IT MEANS A LOT AND HELPS OTHERS JUST LIKE YOU WHO MIGHT ENJOY THIS BOOK, FIND IT TOO.

YOU'RE THE BEST!
FROM ALL OF US WEIRDOS AT BIG DREAMS ART SUPPLIES

Made in the USA
San Bernardino, CA
14 December 2019